FAITH AND DEATH

Questions and Contemplative Answers

Author: Eileen Renders

Eileen Renders is a retired Nutrition and Wellness Counselor specializing in Nutrition, Lifestyle, and Supplements, and has a passion for researching. She is a writer and published author of many titles related to faith, health, and longevity.

Searching For Our Vulnerabilities

Conversing With Jesus

Jesus created a filial relationship between His Mother and us as noted in the bible in **John 19:26-27** when He saw both His mother and His beloved disciple John standing by saying; "Woman, behold your son!" then He said to His beloved disciple John; "Behold thy mother!"

A filial relationship; is a relationship due to a son or daughter, such as in devotion, respect, loyalty, or love. Therefore, if we are disciples and followers of Christ whom Jesus also loves, we too can call the mother of Christ, our mother.

In so doing, Jesus gives us the honor of thinking of Jesus as our Savior, our God, our brother, and our friend. A Savior and creator who loves us so much that He wants us to give love and be loved as family. We must give Jesus the obedience, respect, honor, loyalty, and love that He so much deserves.

Yet, we have also been given the privilege of speaking to Jesus every day as we would our earthly family. Sharing our concerns, sorrows, and confusions that are part of our lives, thanking Him for being there for us in every way, and asking Him to guide us, lead us, and correct us when we are headed in the wrong direction as a big brother would do.

With respect and gratitude for all of God's many blessings, we go to church, we pray Rosaries and Our Father prayers often as we are called to do so. And when we have days, or nights when we are distracted, worried, and want to talk and be assured that God is always there for us listening to our heart's request for comfort, love, and mercy, we can talk to him from the privacy of our hearts and inner thoughts and know that He hears us and truly cares. He wants us to come to Him when we feel heartbroken, lost, or confused.

Sometimes, I like to feel that I pray to our Blessed Mother and offer my prayers up to her to be utilized in her time and for her wishes. I pray to God with honor and gratitude, giving thanks for all His many graces and blessings received throughout my life. But, when I just need to know that He is there listening to me pour my heart out to Him in confidence, I just want to talk to Him.

Basking in God's Glory

Although we have heard the phrase many times, it is still enjoyable to realize the meaning and how it relates to us specifically. God's glory refers to God's goodness, greatness, and indissolubility. We know basking in God's glory, we are delighting in the warmth and comfort of His Light.

How do we then, achieve such a gift from God, and how will we recognize it when it is offered? To begin with, we must first offer up with every prayer to God, our full and sincere submission to His will. When we have surrendered our will to the will of God, we will be serving Him and His people in a way that is most pleasing to God. God's rewards are plentiful!

Recognizing when we are truly basking in the glory of God will be shown and felt by us through an inner warmth, comfortability within ourselves, and a belief that we are living our days doing the will of God.

Again, the first and only prerequisite is that when we make this offering to God, that it is frequent and sincere. We want to make His will our focus. After that, God will accept our offer knowing how it is sincere. He will lead us and provide us with opportunities to share goodwill, and opportunities to assist his people through the talents and words he provides us with. We become a vessel carrying precious cargo, the will of God.

The grace of God will bless us with the knowledge that we are following His will, extending ourselves, our time, and our effort to do good works. And it is

In this spirit of goodwill will we *feel the joy and exhilaration of being in the presence of God.* Through His divine mercy, we are, to say the least, basking in the glory of God, and we cannot help but want every human being to be able to enjoy the treasures that God offers to each one of us.

Jesus Mourns

Our sweet Jesus is in mourning for the souls that have perished and died. He mourns not for those children and souls that have died in love with and trust in him. He mourns for those souls that have perished in the ashes of sin. For they will never again have the opportunity to rise up again and to sin no more for their destiny will be to remain under the domain of Satan, the evil one.

Jesus came to earth after our creation, and after sin came into the world, manipulating our free will. He suffered and died on the Cross in penance for our sins, and before he left us, he created the sacrament of Reconciliation to give us the choice of choosing right from wrong. Jesus wants us all to turn away from evil, and remain free from sin so that we will one day be able to return to him and experience his great love for us.

Our free will is not free as we must pay for our sins against God, and good!

The little souls that die in sickness and through war do not remain dead as we see them last, but they are lifted up in the arms of angels, and delivered to God in whom and where their love was born.

It is only those souls on earth who have been surrounded by the darkness of sin, with heavy black mist clouding their minds and blocking their ability to continue to choose good over evil whom God mourns for. We who remain in the Light of Christ must continue to pray for our brothers and sisters who have lost their way. And always, always remain in gratitude that we who remain in the Light where we can see the wickedness and destruction that accompanies the lies and promises that the evil one utilizes to lure us away from God.

Each day as we meet and greet Christ in prayer with a grateful heart for directing our steps and keeping us safe, let us never forget to pray for all those who have been deceived and have lost their way.

Denying the Darkness of Death

The title of this article may appear to be a bit mystifying as we surely know that we cannot escape the fact that we all must at some time, or another succumb to dying. That is, dying to this earth, to a life that we once lived. If this idea borders on the philosophical, it is meant to do exactly that.

What I want to convey is that in approaching death, it is not that our miraculous body that God created has not surrendered to disease or old age, rather it has heard our creator's call and is willingly and submissively answering that call.

We were all born to parents and a family where we were nurtured and received love. We also learned to return love, and that it is God who sends us love and a unique being born in the likeness of God, our soul.

In First Grade, or before receiving the sacraments Reconciliation and Holy Communion we are taught that God created us for the following reasons; To know Him, love Him, and serve Him in this world so that one day we can be happy with Him in heaven for all eternity.

With that knowledge and understanding, it is good to remember that we are not sliding into the depths of darkness upon our death. No, we are submitting ourselves body and soul into the hands of God. Although our time here is enjoyable and does provide some sense of security, it is important to keep in mind why we were born, and that we are called to live a good life and return to our creator. Accepting death is a way of showing our faith and trust in a God who loves us. Our loved ones will one day join us in our heavenly family for eternity. In showing our trust in God at the time of our departure, we are also solidifying the strength of faith in our loved ones as they witness our acceptance and faith in God's will. For this passing is nothing more than our deliverance, and we are free.

How Might We Be Guilty of Not Sharing the Love of God?

Temptations from the Evil One are often called insidious and cunning and often cause us not to recognize his evil and negativity. Often he tempts not by outright recognizable mortal sins, but in subtle ways that become repetitive and take away from others what is rightfully theirs.

An example might be as follows: Jesus speaks to our hearts and graces us with understanding about how we make choices. In other words; God speaks to your heart and showers you with grace and understanding in a particular matter to one of your loved ones, yet you fail to expound on the very significant importance of that message being that *we all must share* the grace, wisdom and understanding as we know it that has come from God above, then we are probably not the right benefactor for receiving such graces, or blessings from God.

God is love; God is sharing. If we have received a calling to serve Christ through teaching and sharing, and yet desire to keep our relationship and closeness to ourselves, we are not serving God. Just as God shares with those who go to him often, we too must share with others who have yet to understand how to go to Christ, and how much he truly desires our company.

It may be a strong temptation to say to ourselves; "Jesus speaks to me, or Jesus inspires me, I am special to him." That temptation comes from Satan as God does not accept

Pride as it is sinful. Jesus loves and longs for humility in us. To do this for our brothers and sisters because we truly want everyone to give God the love he deserves, and also to feel the love of God within their hearts.

Satan is cunning and baffling and can lure us into turning our weaknesses into sin in trying to raise ourselves up in the process. God is love and mercy, and we are weak, and imperfect, all of us. We were born into sin. The only person born without sin was God's mother. Always keeping the thought within our hearts that the more we give, the more we share, the more God will entrust us with.

What Does God Think About The World Today?

We are living in a time of terrifying, criminal times for young and innocent people, especially God's children. Somehow, we can overlook 195-mile-an-hour winds and fires that destroy 500 homes in a matter of just two days.

Politicians who perjure themselves, and others who fight for dominance and power. We excuse the non-believers simply as those who were just not taught better in their youth and have, therefore, entered adulthood believing that the world was all about themselves.

We, however, are just happy to have found the Living Christ in our everyday lives; we believe in Him, trust in Him, and adore Him. But, once again, we must turn our heads and look over our shoulder and see how HAMAS has murdered thousands of Jews in Israel after years of building underground tunnels, even beneath the floors of a hospital.

We have been witnessing, now for two years or more how Russia is killing the people of Ukraine and destroying their lives. The hunger, the sickness, the terror! America and NATO have responded with aid to Ukraine, still the war rages on.

Now, the Prime Minister of Israel, Benjamin Netanyahu has had revenge for the Israelites. Yet, he will not end the war against HAMAS and is also punishing the Palestinians to such a degree that it is difficult to watch the News as it is delivered to us on Television.

Thousands of sick and elderly of GAZA are dying without shelter, medicine, or a hospital. Children are dying of famine. Evil surrounds us. The United States thus far has been unable to influence Israel to cease fire because of the humanitarian crisis. Russia is again talking about sending a nuclear weapon into the sky near the Western part of the world.

While millions are dying at the hands of evil power-seeking leaders, and children are dying by the hundreds of famine, it is those millions of people who are unperturbed by all of this because it does not affect their little world, that is the most upsetting aspect of all.

It is time now, I believe that we might ask ourselves, "How does our God Almighty feel about all of this?" Our God is a caring, loving God who created each one of us. Could God somehow be allowing more time for change? Could our loving, merciful God be able to overlook the slaughter of small, innocent children day after day? I believe you and I can agree that it could not be possible.

Therefore, we might expect to look up to heaven and in just a few weeks see a sign from God, a true Warning from our creator of the world. Could it be that Satan's time for roaming the world and convincing people to follow him is over? Could it be nearing the time of the Second coming of Christ? Do we feel that it is not justified as our world is moving along satisfactorily? Have we become oblivious to the suffering of others, are we complacent?

My emotions were followed by a letter to the White House for a National Day of Prayer for Peace. We have Presidents' Day, Martin Luther King Day, a Saint Patrick's Day, but it is politically incorrect to mention God. How very sad, and a possible predictor of what we all may be witnessing in the days to come, our creator.

Prayer, repentance, and remaining in the state of grace is our only defense.

The Energy of Creation

As curious creatures, we seek the many answers to such
questions as how and why. Our capabilities are limited, yet
our ability and energy for reaching out and seeking answers
to our questions seem to be endless.

For the most part, it appears that our creator placed us
humans on earth through the energy of love. A precious
thought, a gift. Because our energy is limited, and housed
within the confines of a limited time frame, we must reach
out beyond our limitations to the One who has created us
out of love, and to pray for knowledge and understanding of
the mysteries that often consume our thoughts.

Our questions about life here on earth are often similar,
such as; If God created us through His energy and love for
us, why then is there evil that exists within the dark corners
of this earth? Why did we inherit the Father's ability to
love, and then be tortured by seeing loved ones suffer and
die, to leave us feeling somewhat abandoned? Why does
our mate for life through the sacrament of Marriage dismiss
us for the affection of a new love? And why do little

children suffer and die when their lives have barely just begun? The questions are endless, but the answers seemingly evade us.

And if our God made us through the energy of His love, why do we continue to suffer in this temporary world? Is this world meant to be a puzzle that each one of us must work to solve by putting it all together in a manner that makes sense and satisfies us?

It is apparent that what we have learned through Jesus' teachings in that brief period when He inhabited this earth with us, is that evil also roams the world seeking the destruction of God's creation, we, His people. Whether it is an added gift or something beyond our capabilities, God gave us free will to choose our path in life. Although our free will is a positive gift and allows us to choose what is right in life, evil follows our very footsteps, lies to us, and tempts us to make bad choices. Life can be very difficult, especially for those with mental, and or physical disabilities as our weaknesses can cause some of us to collapse into a state of misery that is combined with distrust, self-pity, and disregard for God.

How then do we navigate this world in such a way that we gain the respect and reward of our Creator through the choices we make throughout our lives? The answer is always right there within us, no it is not always what we want, nor what we choose, however, God did not leave us without the Light of His grace that He laid out for us in His own words through the Ten Commandments.

What is clear and true for all of us is that in choosing what is right and of God, regardless of how much sorrow, and how much pain is involved in making good choices, this is what we must do to be graced and blessed with the gifts of wisdom, tolerance, understanding, love, and mercy. And in following His path, our creator who suffered and died because of our wrong choices (sins), we might also one day rise above our imperfections to be greeted by Christ and remain with Him in Heaven for all eternity! This choice to follow Christ, and suffer our temporary crosses and roadblocks, might even be considered a "no-brainer" choice toward our endless reward.

Why Do Only Some Have an Intimate Relationship with Jesus?

Here is a question that most likely resonates with all of us at one time or another: "Why do some people have a much closer relationship with Jesus than others?" Some of us may have even wondered if God has chosen favorites as his friends. A couple of considerations regarding this subject matter are important to our understanding.

When Jesus was born to his mother, he walked the earth as we do, he had Saint Joseph as a Stepfather, and the Blessed Virgin Mary as his mother. He grew up most probably helping his stepfather in his Carpentry Shop, and completing chores as requested by his parents.

As Jesus grew and matured, he went about his Father in heaven's work and spent time in the Temple learning and teaching. When Jesus called upon the Apostles to follow him, the Gospels often depicted John, James, and Peter having been his favorites. We do know that it was these three whom Jesus asked to follow him up to a mountain to pray, and there they witnessed the Transfiguration.

In understanding who Jesus is, we must realize that his love, protection, and mercy is equal to all of his creatures. One way to explain how and why Jesus may have spent more time with John, James, and Peter is that it was they who were always by his side, wanting to hear more, ask questions, and comfort and support him.

An example of how that might work in our own families is to imagine grandparents who live near their grown children and their grandchildren. Suppose they had eight grandchildren, and three grandchildren, especially like to go to Grandma's and spend time there. In turn, they share meals with their grandparents and listen to many stories of days gone by that they find very interesting and entertaining. This might explain why they may have a more intimate relationship with their grandparents, and exclude the idea that the grandparents chose them to be favorites.

In our lifetime, we can still nurture an intimate relationship with Jesus. We do this just as the Apostles did, in following His commandments, attending Mass, praying, and always talking to Him and seeking answers from Him. Would we then not be more intimate with Jesus than those who simply go to Sunday Mass and say a few prayers now, and again?

God, Can You Hear Me?

Jesus Speaks through the Holy Spirit

How often have we heard about the "Ups and Downs" of life? As an adolescent, those words reminded me of some Amusement ride in a Park. Entering adulthood, leaving my parents, and embarking on a future of my choosing, I began to understand the meaning of those words I had heard long ago. Life, of course, has its joyous occasions, and opportunities, and many dreams are realized.

However, we also experience illness, failure, and disappointments, and begin to lose some of the family we loved so much. Too often, we are tempted to believe that we are being punished for being disobedient to God. This feeling can spiral into fear, anxiety, or depression. The truth of the matter is that it is sin that separates us from God.

Whenever we choose to go our own way and do whatever seems to promise us enjoyment, gratification, or financial success, it is we who willfully choose to turn away from

God and His Commandments. God sent His only son Jesus Christ to come down on earth to teach us to live according to His will and to avoid the snares of Satan whose sole desire is to separate us from God. His purpose was not to punish us but to save us!

Therefore, when we pray to God and our prayers are not answered, rather than take that silence as a rejection, and often due to a feeling of worthlessness, we might reflect upon this time of silence. There is a message that we are not hearing.

It may be that we need to accept the reality of our life, the negative feelings we are experiencing are the result of our choices. We must bear our Cross as we all must accept our Crosses in life. More importantly, we might want to rethink our initial conclusions, such as God is punishing us for our sins. God died a very degrading and painful death for the love of us. Therefore, when we feel the stillness and chill of being separated from God, He has not left us; it is we who have left Him!

God desires nothing more than to forgive us and bring us back into the fold. He is the good Shepherd.

Feeling abandoned by God often is the result of abandoning Him through sin. It causes us to feel unworthy of God's love, and we turn our backs on Him. In this quiet time of our lives when we are experiencing those "Down" times when everything seems to be falling apart, we need not hide those feelings from Him.

Always, we ought to remember that Jesus' love for us never fails. We need only to confess our sorrow for having hurt Him. Gratefully pick up our cross with courage and most of all, with trust that God is watching and wants what is best for us. The Holy Spirit can enlighten your heart when you spend time with God in honesty and faith in His love for all of us.

Contemplating Our Health and God's Guidance

As we approach each new day, remember to give thanks to God for this new day, and pray each evening before retiring, for God's protection, we are placing our trust in him. In so doing, we are saying that we desire to follow his lead and guidance in each step we take along life's journey.

If this last statement is true, then it makes sense that we would be wise to read his word often for His guidance. His elected Apostles, knowing that he would not always be with them, nor would they always be walking on earth, took care to write down God's word, which can be found in our bible.

As long as we remain on earth, our health is important in many ways. Most of us are required to work, and we need energy to work and serve the Lord well. Therefore, I want to call to mind one of the ways that God's word has set me on my path in life as a Wellness Consultant, and as one who serves God through my writing is a direct result of God's grace and blessings.

With an inner trust for God's word, the following bible passages have stuck with me throughout life. This is not to say that I do not believe in medicine or surgery, not at all. However, after being enlisted by the Atlantic City Medical Center in Atlantic City, New Jersey to work with the HIV of two Counties, funded from funding known as The Ryan White Program through the National Institutes of Health, because a young boy, Ryan White contracted HIV through an unclean needle from a dentist, and later died.

I worked with HIV because a 5-year Study revealed that some learned Herbs and Nutrients could be beneficial to HIV individuals (not a program for those with full-blown AIDS). In working with these HIV individuals, I noted how the drugs used to treat HIV were difficult for their bodies to handle. As a result, they presented with inflamed livers, nausea, insomnia, and headache, all of which they received another script for. In my work, I was able to eliminate secondary drugs through recommendations that were without side effects for headache, nausea, etc. This in turn, removed some of the toxic effects that were going on within their bodies and their livers.

Note: Many drugs are derived from herbs; however, they go through a breakdown in their molecular structure through processing to produce a more potent drug, one that can be branded.

Digitalis (a heart medication) comes from the herb Foxglove

Taxol (a chemotherapy drug) is isolated from the bark of the Pacific Yew tree

White willow bark has been utilized and processed into Aspirin

Red Yeast Rice (an effective herb) works well with some individuals to maintain a healthy HDL cholesterol, and is how Statins were manufactured, which very often can cause side effects.

Needless to say, there are many other examples, such as Frankincense and Myrrh. And much more than I can write herein.

All from the word of God!

Bible quotes

Mathew Chapter 7:12 (The New International Bible)

Jesus said; "so in everything, do to others what you would have them do to you."

John 13:34-35

Jesus said; "A new command I give to you; Love one another as I have loved you, so you must love one another. By this, everyone will know that you are my Disciples, if you love one another."

Genesis 1:29 (King James) also in **Ezekiel 47:12**

And God said; "Behold, I have given you every herb bearing seed, which is upon the face

Of the earth, every tree, which is the fruit of a tree yielding seed; to you, it shall be for meat."

On each bank of the stream, all kinds of trees will grow to provide food. Their leaves will never wither and they will never stop bearing fruit. They will have fresh fruit every month because they are watered by the stream that flows from the temple.

Arise and Awaken

Being Glad for Our Creator Loves Us

We have so much to be thankful for this Easter because we are loved greatly by our loving and merciful God. It was His desire here on earth to teach us by His example to love one another as He has loved us. Avoid false pride by judging others.

Let us review the Seven deadly sins so that each day we may examine our conscience and become aware of our weaknesses so that we can gain strength through Christ to overcome our weaknesses and be in tune with the subtle temptations he whispers into our hearts each day.

Focus on the Beatitudes as they encourage us to emulate the martyrs and Saints. Not so much that we may be called to become a martyr, or to become a Saint as we are not working to attain adulation or recognition, but to become pleasing to God.

Here are the Seven Deadly Sins

Pride ~ Boasting of our accomplishments, or judging others as being less accomplished as oneself. We need to frequently remind ourselves that all of our energies, intellect, and talents come from God and are not what we may have deserved or earned ourselves.

Covetousness ~ This is a sin of greed, an insatiable desire for more than we have, and never feeling grateful, or satisfied with what we have.

Lust ~ Lust is a constant, or continual focus on sexual thoughts and desires. This sin takes away all healthy and spiritual thoughts of God. It removes all thoughts of goodness and kindness as God does not share space or time in the darkness of sin.

Anger ~ This is a sin of hostility, annoyance, and inability to rationality, understanding, love, or mercy. It can often even lead to injuring another human being.

Gluttony ~ This is a sin of wanting excess of more than one's needs, or a proportionate share of something. Oftentimes, it is food always eaten to excess.

Envy ~ This sin is usually associated with an ongoing feeling of dissatisfaction with what one has, or owns. And always looking at what others have, or wanting their possessions that are never rightfully theirs.

Sloth ~ This is a sin of laziness, it is an individual wanting all that others have without working for those needs, and possessions, and without deserving what they feel they should be given.

The Eight Beatitudes

With the 8 Beatitudes, we learn about the poor in spirit, those who mourn, the meek, those who hunger and thirst for righteousness, the merciful, the pure in heart, the peacemakers, and those persecuted for the sake of righteousness. It is good, for all to work toward becoming better people for the love of God.

Hauntings from the Past

As we mature, grow, and age, we often find that in those times, when we are feeling low due to sickness, disappointment, or other not-so-positive issues, we backtrack and reflect on our beginnings in life and in particular, when we embarked on our independent journey to find out exactly who we are. As we grow into adulthood we recognize that we are often changing our perspectives and priorities. Of course, these feelings can present a bit of confusion and insecurities. We may become centered on a quest to discover what it is we like about ourselves and what we desire to change about ourselves.

As the years pass and as we age, science tells us it is our long-term memory that will remain with us into old age. Our short-term memory quickly fades and involves a different storage compartment within our brain.

Therefore, this reflection that takes us further back into the past than we sometimes would rather not go can stir up some of our many unpleasant memories. I am referring to those times when we may have said, thought, or done something we truly regret.

Although we may have made the sacrament of Reconciliation sincerely, and know that we have received absolution and God has forgiven us. If God loves us so much to forgive us of our sins, why can we not forgive ourselves?

These negative feelings can lead to self-loathing. Most importantly we must live in today, this moment, and recognize that without forgiving ourselves of our past mistakes we stir up emotions of unworthiness of God's love. These feelings separate us from God. There is not one of us sinners on this earth that is worthy of God's love as we were all born into life with original sin.

One positive way of accepting our imperfections is to consider this thought that I propose to you, and it goes like this; "Life is not so much about where we came from, or who we are today, it is much more about who we are becoming!"

In retrospect, it is very often easy to see our faults and mistakes, but understanding that when we made the biggest wrong choices in our lives, some may have been hurting, seeking acceptance, being wrongfully influenced, or even thoughtfully manipulated into not seeing too clearly our choices, and the consequences of those choices. If we truly have learned from our poor choices and have become stronger disciples of Christ, we have moved to higher ground, and we are showing God that He is now the focus and priority in our lives.

With our newfound spirituality, it is wise to leave the negativity of one's past where it belongs, in the past. We only have today.

Triumph Over Defeat

Similar to the paradox of how surrendering is often the answer to setting one free, so also might this concept apply to "Turning the other cheek". Moreover, allowing our hearts to remain open and loving after we have been deceived and hurt by a loved one whom we had placed our trust in.

In reviewing our choices, we can allow feelings of hatred, rejection, or revenge to harden our hearts and shut the door of our hearts to trust anyone again in the future. Or, we can turn the other cheek, forgive one's offenses toward us, and show mercy. This latter choice allows us to seek goodness in our lives, go out on a limb, and again extend trust and mercy.

Sometimes, we ask ourselves "Why should I trust again, I learned my lesson." Yet this is exactly the attitude that festers and grows dark within our spirit, creating an unpathetic being that seeks respect, honesty, and appreciation that they can no longer extend to another.

Life has a way, however, of returning the same type of energy that we project. Therefore, we can reap little love from others, nor a sense of "belonging", or "fitting in."

Always looking at Christ as our example and as our guide, we know how He gave His all to save us by His acceptance of His persecutors' sentencing of His painful Crucifixion. He accepted our rejection of Him, our disbelief in Him, and surrendered His life to a humiliating and most painful death on the Cross. His sacrifice allowed us to follow His example and save our souls. Jesus did indeed triumph over defeat. In accepting this fate as His Father in heaven asked of Jesus, He has shown us how to accept the errors of others and forgive.

It is quite natural to struggle with forgiving as it often is only done without forgetting the hurt and pain we endured, and then forgave. Like our Father in heaven, however, forgiving does not require that we accept that individual back into our arms and spend time with them. We can see this in God because we have learned that the wicked and deceitful who refuse to repent and live a life that respects

His Ten Commandments are told that we will also not be welcomed into the arms of Christ when our life here on earth has expired.

We are asked to pray for all who need prayer for conversion, that they too may one day look forward to the eternity God offers to all who follow His word.

What Jesus Taught Us by His Example

In contemplating the life that Jesus lived as a Carpenter's son on earth and preparing as He matured, to complete the task of His ministry of teaching His sheep and dying on the Cross to save us from the snares of Satan, He provided many lessons to us regarding clean and healthy living.

He showed us how He remained obedient to His Mother Mary, and His stepfather St. Joseph, He showed us the graces associated with humility. Jesus practiced the Beatitudes as well. Jesus avoided envy, sloth, and gluttony.

Whenever we are unsure of how to proceed in a particular situation or in making an important decision, we may ask ourselves as I often do, "What would Jesus do?" Let us not forget that Jesus taught us also how to remain healthy of body, mind, and spirit.

For example, cancer was stable in the United States between 1909 and 1918. When World War 1 ended in 1918, and then in 1919 we saw an increase in cancer of 6.6%. World War 11 ended with the surrender of Germany in 1945.

Chicago established itself in the early 1900s as the meat packaging center in the United States, and then along came refrigeration, all of which created the opportunity for every family to partake daily in the consumption of beef and pork.

The greatest rise in the early onset of cancers, including esophagus, breast, liver, and pancreas was noted globally in the early 1900s. Today research tells us that red meat is highly acidic and changes the body's ideal pH range. Those of us who own a swimming pool or fish tank are aware of the importance of a safe pH balance for health and survival.

Our pH range is ideal between 7.2 – 7.4, slightly alkaline. This is best for ideal oxygenation of blood. We are composed of two-thirds water.

To return once again to Jesus and how He taught us. Jesus, from all that we have noted in bible verses, sat down for a meal consisting of fresh fish, baked bread, and a small glass of wine or water.

We depend today on refrigeration, highly processed foods, and excess intake of red meat, salt, or excess sugar, not at all the way our Creator lived and ate. The paradox of the sweetness of sugar is that it, too, is highly acidic.

From 1990 forward, due to modernization, we are seeing the highest increase in cancers such as the esophagus, breast, and liver.

Back in the day, people were not always dependent upon medications for everything from the flu to high cholesterol to obesity. Many physical conditions can often be reversed under a physician's care through regular exercise and good nutrition. For over twenty years I have tried to follow God's lead through research and writing of health books and always with Christ at the center.

Be Not Afraid

There are at least three instances in the Catholic bible where the phrase "Be Not Afraid" is mentioned. They are contained in the Catholic Bible and are contained in verses from Matthew, Genesis, Luke, and John.

In **Luke 12:32** Jesus says, "Do not be afraid, little flock, for your Father has been pleased to give you the Kingdom."

Luke 2:10: At the birth of Jesus, the angel announces to the shepherds, "Be not afraid; for behold, I bring you news of great joy."

In **Genesis 26:24** The Lord appears to Isaac and reassures him, saying, "I am with you and will bless you, do not be afraid."

Genesis 15:1: The Lord speaks to Abram (later known as Abraham) and says, "Do not be afraid, Abram, I am your shield; your reward will be very great."

In **Matthew 10:26:** Jesus instructs His disciples, "So have no fear of them; for nothing is covered up that will not be uncovered, and nothing secret that will not become known."

Matthew 10:28: He further emphasizes, "Do not fear those who kill the body but cannot kill the soul; rather fear Him who can destroy both soul and body in hell."

Matthew 28:5-6: After Jesus' resurrection, the angel tells the women at the tomb, "Do not be afraid, for I know that you are looking for Jesus, who was crucified. He is not here; He has risen."

And again in John 14:27: Jesus says, "Peace I leave you; my peace I give unto you: not as the world gives. Let not your heart be troubled, nor let it be afraid."

John 14:1-3: Jesus comforts His disciples by saying: "Let not your hearts be troubled, Believe in God; believe also in me. In my Father's house, there are many rooms. If it were not so, would I have told you that I go to prepare a place for you? And if I go and prepare a place for you, I will come again, and will take you to myself, that where I am you may be also. And you know the way to where I am going."

- This beautiful promise reminds us how Jesus goes ahead of us, preparing a heavenly dwelling place for those who trust in Him. It's a message of hope, assurance, and eternal comfort.

These verses by Jesus' faithful disciples, who grew to know Jesus intimately, carry the most important message to all of us that by our very trust in Jesus, our faith is sealed, and we are protected. In the philosophy of life, it is very evident that trust is the opposite of fear. Fear then can destroy us, while faith can save us.

Living In The Present

For many reasons, sometimes dissatisfaction, or expectations, we tend to think of the future as the answer to our dreams come true. This can cause us to dismiss our past experiences and what lessons we may have learned from them as we look to the future.

Keeping hope in our everyday thoughts, and nourishing the faith within our hearts and souls, is addressing our stability and freeing our spirits for an eternity one day in heaven with Christ when He whispers our name saying, "Come to Me."

However, it is essential to our daily reality to live today as tomorrow will come soon enough. By living today, we can see and properly deal with those issues, be they small or large, that require our immediate attention. Each day as we arise, is a good time to reflect upon those we love, and who may be ill, and need a little loving support. Often, we can overlook those subtle words of a friend who is struggling to pay the Bills as he or she has lost their job. Can we afford to make a worthy donation and kind words of support? Have we taken a few moments to tell God that we love Him and ask Him to remain with us throughout the day, and have we thanked our spouse for their unending love and support?

There can be no tomorrow without a today. And it is how we live each day God gives us that will provide a better tomorrow for each of us. This is true because we will have a deeper relationship with Christ and a better understanding and acceptance of the possibility that none of us is promised a "tomorrow."

The happiest and most contented people on earth are those who are happy and content with what they have. Those who are always seeking more seem never to be satisfied, or content. Consider that each of our lives is in part, a testament of who we are at the core. Do we seek to serve others for the joy of God's blessings and graces, or do we long to achieve success and acknowledgment from others around us? Do we need to be looked up to for what we have gained?

We all can attest to how good it feels when we are able to give at Christmas and see the joy and pleasure we can give to someone else. When we do good for the sake of others, God refills our cup so that we may continue to give.

It is wise, however, to keep in mind that life is truly a test, an opportunity to prepare ourselves for our exit from this life. And who among us does not wish for a peaceful death feeling the very presence of God beside us, ready to take us home to paradise?

Is Jesus Still Here?

As a child in elementary Catholic School, and in preparation for receiving our first Sacraments, we learned that Jesus was omnipresent, meaning He could see all, hear all, and know all. However, curious to me, I did not see that kind of acknowledgment growing up around me. Adults seemed to project that God was someone whom we must deal with at some point before we die, and the present was for dealing with life here on earth. I did not understand that at all. I expected adults especially, to be more aware of God's presence in the world. Still, I heard cursing, I saw people in the neighborhood often arguing, and other behavior that I found to be against God's Commandments.

I wondered. Did they not believe that God could see and hear them? Today, I marvel at some of the concepts of young people that we hear our parents say about their children who participate in an intimate live-in situation saying, "Oh no, they are not getting married right now, millennials don't get married right away." Implying that this new way of thinking is much more adaptable and eliminates the risk of making a mistake that might end in divorce. Marriage does not allow a couple in love to be able to avoid that period of adjustment, nor does it prevent disagreements or financial difficulties. Marriage is a commitment, not a feeling.

The Bible states that man was lonely, and God created woman. God provided the two sexes for procreation, and only under the sacrament of Marriage. A young couple living together is not an option for "sampling" to see if it feels right. Many young couples are recommended by the Catholic Church, to attend Marriage Counseling before getting married. Psychologists will affirm that when sex enters into a relationship before a couple has had the time to first focus on a potential partner's beliefs regarding God, church, marriage, children, and finances, to see whether or not they may be compatible, the relationship is already doomed.

Too, this type of coupling is entered into without a mature understanding, or commitment can also affect any future relationships, especially for a young woman. Women are meant to be respected and held in high esteem. Men may see a woman who has several failed relationships without a legal or religious commitment are not right for them.

Making wise decisions in one's life is best not thought of as rules or constraints but as directions proven to lead us toward happiness and success, and more importantly, in living a pleasing way God has taught us to live.

Are We A "Doubting Thomas?

How joyfully surprised were the Apostles when they heard that Christ had risen? Jesus came down upon them in the upper room to console them. However, Thomas said that if He could touch Him, he could not fully believe Christ had risen.

Jesus allowed Thomas to approach and touch Him saying, "Blessed are those who believe and have not seen, for theirs is the Kingdom of heaven." Because it is not written, it is quite common for us to wonder exactly what happens next after our death. We believe in Three persons in one God as Jesus taught us when He was here with us on earth. We were taught and we believe that God is, always was and always will be, which is difficult for us humans to comprehend. Faith, however, is our armor, and it wards off doubt and confusion.

Perhaps when Jesus was on earth for thirty-three years preparing for His sacrifice on the Cross, and teaching in the Temple, and at the same time selecting His Apostles to watch and listen to what He was saying and doing so that they could continue His Teachings, and writing for the Bible to come forth that Jesus performed so many miracles as it was very important that His Disciples know and believe who sent Him.

Jesus said to His followers, "I go to the Father, and where I AM, so too will you be with Me." Jesus also said, "In My Father's house there are many rooms, I go before you to prepare a place for you." This last sentence in some ways conjures up the idea that we who do make it to heaven may have very different Quarters there. For example, Some of us are very serious animal lovers, and perhaps where we are, so too will there be all our pets we once owned. For others who love music, perhaps they will have a special place to relax and listen to beautiful music. Others may consider beautiful Flower Gardens to sit by, and they, too will have a garden next to their Quarters.

Have you ever asked yourself how God, with billions of people, could hear each one of us as we pray and speak to Him? And how did He name thousands of Stars and know each one by name? God is Omnipresent; He can be in many places at the same time. Perhaps, in heaven, that is exactly how He will be able to be with all of us.

Of course, we do not have all the answers, but we do recognize that whatever God gives us is all good. Therefore, it is just the trust that we have in Him that allows us to look forward to our life after death.

Being with someone as death nears can be a very remarkable experience. One of my family members spoke to his wife briefly before death and told her that he had seen a beautiful gold Carriage coming to take him home. Death can be frightening for many reasons, such as seeing or hearing of a violent death, or the much suffering one must endure before dying. More often than not, however, doctors and nurses who have seen many dying deny seeing patients die in pain or with fear.

Preparing for our departure is sometimes a good way to prioritize and direct our prayers to God, asking for more trust and a peaceful death.

Tangling With Depression

What causes depression, and are healthy, active people likely to be struck down by depression? In my opinion, to address those questions, it is fair to say that some degrees and variables have a definite bearing on answers. For example, the level of activity in one's life may affect the degree and/or the longevity of one's depression. Another influence on one's ability to recover from depression could be one's age. The stability of one's faith can also be critical in the recovery from depression, as it is tied to the trust and hope that is part of our stability. When there is a neurological issue that requires addressing, it is wise to visit a Specialist. Our Creator does not want us to suffer, He is loving and merciful.

It is comforting to be reminded that Pharmacologists, Scientists, and Medical doctors may have been led by God to pursue their careers because they wanted to serve God by helping others.

Therefore, each of us is individually different from one another in our lifestyle, age, and degree of faith. The life we live in ensuring our health, our lifestyle, and our activity, or community involvement, is critical to one's recovery of most aspects of our psychological and physiological ability to rebound after a setback.

While many individuals have not expressed or practiced faith in their lives, they may have taken care to include sound nutrition as their primary concern for themselves. This does not in any way assume that they have also included a healthy consistent activity in their lives as well. Also, what might occur in the same situation for seniors who are unable to participate in a consistent healthy exercise program? We have not even presented the idea of genetics, which can also play a major role in determining a role in one's longevity.

It turns out this simple single question that was presented at the beginning of this writing has sort of turned into a quagmire of variables that must address each sector of people separately with different solutions.

To keep it simple, I offer a reflection from a retired Nutritionist, Health research writer, and author who is a senior; healthy seniors might consider part-time work, pursuing their hobbies, or taking up some charitable volunteer work. Others, who may be older seniors with limited abilities, might decide upon senior group travel events, church activities, focusing on health, and we all could use more God in our lives regardless of religious beliefs. When we give God the time and love He deserves, He always gives back. It may not always be what we want from Him; however, He knows best what we need.

Is The Soul Recognizable?

Is the soul invisible? If it is, then surely only God could recognize our souls. So, this question might be important to only you and me. For we die in the state of grace and are only reunited with our bodies when Christ comes again, only our souls arise into heaven until reunited with our bodies. This being the truth as it has been told and written, surely then our souls will be recognizable to all our family and friends who have gone before us.

How we will be recognizable to one another deserves some consideration. My opinion is based on the fact that there have been many spiritual and miraculous apparitions throughout the ages, which have mostly been described as visions of God, or His Blessed Mother in the cloud-like form of beings that were distinguishable, yet almost see-through. Children could liken that type of vision to Casper the friendly ghost.

Seeing God in the flesh as He is in the beatific vision, as described by Thomas Aquinas, was defined as the human being's "end" in which one attains to perfect happiness. We have been told that our eyes would be unable to view God as He really is because it would be too much glory and light for our eyes to behold.

In heaven, as we await God's final return to earth, and before we are reunited with our earthly bodies that are being purified, I believe that we have a sort of recognizable form that is without flesh and blood. After Christ's finale to earth returns and Satan is cast into hell forever, only then will the Final Judgement take place. Those who have lived faithfully to God's Commandments and are in a state of grace will be taken up to heaven. Those souls in heaven awaiting their bodies will be reunited with their bodies once again. Those who lived a violent, unholy life and belong to Satan will be sentenced to hell forever with Satan.

Much of this information is contained within the pages of the Catholic bible, and some of it is not very clear. However, I believe we all feel that the end result of our destiny is very similar to what is outlined in this article. Since there is no relevance placed on time when we are in heaven, it doesn't matter how long it takes.

What Drives You?

Needless to say, as young adults, we are all motivated in ways that will provide some security for our future, including investigating those faraway places that intrigue us, and leave ample time for continuing education, friends, and hobbies. As young adults, our energy is most likely at its highest. With so many thoughts of personal goals, there is often little time for the rest our bodies require.

Our priorities are often quite different of younger individuals in many ways. Looking back as more mature individuals, we might note that most of our motives were self-centered. Sadly, we may have placed Jesus lower on our list of priorities, as though there would be time enough for Him when we are settled in with our lives, have more time on our hands, or possibly experience defeats, losses, or health issues. That kind of attitude is much like saying; "When I need Him, I will go to Him." Sadly, this example is passed down to our children.

Realizing our preoccupation with ourselves requires a making up for lost time and reconciliation with our Lord and Master, God! We may begin to feel remorseful, and this is a sign of acknowledgment to God of our sorrow, and He deserves our apologies. He is so loving that it is never too late to realize the error of our ways, and with our sincerity and focus on Him, we can be forgiven.

In those quiet times when we are alone with our thoughts, we may be reliving the blessed times we spent with a good friend, or even a parent we have lost through an illness. All of which, reminds us that we have already lived a good portion of our lives and we can only count on one day at a time. In delving into the dark depths of death, perhaps a chapter of our lives that we avoided believing it was so far into the future that there was no sense in being morbid.

Sadly, however, we all see young people dying as well as older folks. Truthfully, death is not a pleasant thought for any of us because it requires us to give up our comfortable homes, our loved ones, and all of our treasured memories and contacts. We may wonder; "What is really in the beyond, on the other side?" This is especially true for those who are a bit late in contemplating the idea of how they need and want the comfort and love of God.

Again, this realization in itself is a first step toward getting closer to our Creator. We can still get down on our knees and sincerely apologize for lost time. More importantly, we must prove our sincerity in making Him our priority in life through prayer, meditation, frequenting the sacraments, and living to serve only Him by following His Commandments and being a good example to all whom you come in contact with.

The Meaning of Life

This philosophical question, "What is the meaning of Life"? deserves contemplation, and can be answered in many different ways depending upon who is answering. Realizing that some individuals who favor a scientific view might believe that life is meant to propagate so that life continues.

Others may feel that life is each individual's opportunity to achieve, to acquire recognition and success, so that they may feel fulfilled and the end of their lives. Many might believe that life is given to each of us, and we might seek and find happiness and joy throughout our days.

We, however, who are Catholic, know that the purpose of our lives is to live according to God's will and to resist holding on to our will. As we begin to realize at some point in our lives that our will is often filled with selfish or poorly influenced choices. We have learned that our lives will always be a bit restless or anxious until we open the door of our hearts, allowing God to come in and guide us along the way.

Because God has given us free will is evidence that we can either choose right or wrong. We need to place Him first in our lives. Yes, God wants to be first in our lives, He created us. Only when we *do* place Him first in our lives can we fully understand His motivation. It is not that God demands to be first in our life; He has given us free will. It is not that His love is selfish; on the contrary, God cannot give us what He desires to give us until He has our attention, love, and devotion. This may be because he wants to ensure that we will use His gifts in the best manner.

God's gifts are given individually according to each of us in a manner that will serve Him through serving others. In the **Gospel of Matthew, chapter 25,** Jesus speaks about the importance of compassion and kindness toward others.

In Matthew:40 "And the King shall answer and say unto them, verily I say unto you, since ye have done it unto one of the least of these My brethren, ye have done unto me."

Not one of us can give to God without being rewarded tenfold. Keeping in mind, of course, our gifts, sacrifices, prayers, or serving God must be done with pure sincerity, or it is like an empty box wrapped nicely.

A Prayer to Jesus From Our Heat and Soul

Jesus, Jesus, You are the One,

Sent from the Father, His only Son

Jesus, Jesus, You are the One.

Together with the Holy Spirit, three persons in One.

Jesus, Jesus. Where you are is where I want to be.

Let me not stray from thee.

Jesus, Jesus, I live to remain sin-free, to be obedient,

And with You, I want to be for all eternity.

Jesus, Jesus, You are my friend,

You promise to be with me until my life comes to an end.

Jesus, Jesus, thank you for always being there,

I promise to trust in you forever.

Jesus, Jesus, I will leave you never.

Jesus, Jesus, I am yours.

We Are Saved One Day At A Time

We are all aware that our Lord and Savior, our Creator, Jesus Christ, died on the Cross to save us from our sins. Yet many times, I have heard people say, "I am saved, Christ died on the cross for our sins." This phrase seems to be a bit deficient from reality as it seems to indicate that one believes he, or she is going directly to heaven when they die because Christ died on the Cross for our sins, and to save us.

If we believe this, we may be missing the true meaning of Jesus' sacrifice. God sent His only son to earth to eventually be crucified to save His people from hell. We were all born with original sin, except the chosen mother of Christ, the Blessed Virgin Mary, who was born without sin, and who conceived Jesus Christ in her womb through the power of the Holy Spirit.

Through Jesus Christ, our sins were removed and forgiven, however, that does not mean that any or all of our future sins are automatically forgiven. This is why Jesus created the sacraments of Reconciliation, Matrimony, Holy Communion, Baptism, and Extreme Unction, or the Last Rites. Should we die in sin, we will all be judged. Some will go to Purgatory for a cleansing of the soul, others who die in the state of grace may go right to heaven, and those unfortunate who did not frequent the sacraments, express sorrow to God and seek forgiveness in the Confessional may go to hell.

God is our Creator, our Savior, and our ultimate judge. How do we best live our lives? We have learned by example from the saints that living our lives through loving Christ, serving Christ, and following His Ten Commandments is the best way to find God's mercy in the final hour. Though we live our lives following Jesus, none of us could ever be worthy of gaining entrance card blanche into heaven as that occurs only through the love and mercy of God.

In Conquering Sin, We Create A Temple for The Lord

In contemplating the subject matter of this article's title, it may sound like one of those suggestions whereby many may respond by saying or thinking, "Easier said than done." However, determined in our efforts in many areas of our lives. For example; we have learned how to be steadfast in pursuing that perfect job for ourselves, we have learned how to practice good nutrition along with regular exercise to become healthier, we have been patient and focused in finding that mate that is right for us, and compliments who we are.

Why then, are we often losing the battle against sin? Time and again, committing the same repetitive sins! God Himself is relentless in His effort to pursue us and bring us closer to Him. As Catholics, we practice Reconciliation, receive the body and blood of Christ, and then we leave the church to go out and once again give in to the act of sin.

As we learned as children before making our first sacraments, for an act to be a sin, we must think about this sin, realize that it is a sin (and hurts God), and then commit that sin regardless of the consequences. Possibly some of us go to the sacrament of Reconciliation without sincerity, or thinking to ourselves, "I will try not to do that again." This type of thinking truly sets us up for failure. It comforts us and allows us to sin because subliminally we are telling ourselves that it is too difficult to resist sin as we are only human.

In reflection, we may realize that, unlike securing a position at work or finding the right mate through determination or patience, relinquishing Satan's hold on us requires more from us. We need to spend more time with Him in silence thinking about how we hurt Him time, and time again. Knowing how we are letting down our creator who loves us will soon create empathy and appreciation, and our love for Him will grow. So much so that we become fighters against sin for the love of God comes first in our lives.

Remaining dedicated to understanding how we hurt Christ daily through sin and spending more time with Him will help us grow in our love for Him, and Christ will grace us with the fortitude to resist sin. When we commit to a lifetime partner in Marriage, we never want to be hurt or hurt them through the sin of adultery. Why then do we stray from Christ and give in to Satan? The more we resist sin, the more graces and blessings God bestows upon us. We must commit to Him first in our daily lives. A promise, to relinquish weak thoughts such as "I will *try* not to sin again.

A Soul Departs the Body Embarking Upon A Three-Day Journey Into The Dark Abyss

We have learned through Christ's time and teachings while on earth, that though He must leave us, He sends to us The Holy Spirit. Jesus left behind His life on earth after completing His Father's request. Jesus' mission was to teach, and ultimately sacrifice His life through His crucifixion and death on the cross. We were given free will to choose good, or evil. God, or Satan.

We have learned that when we die, our soul leaves the body, and will be judged according to the choices we have made in our lives, and whether or not we die in the state of grace. Jesus also promised that at the end of time of times when He returns once more to earth, all will be judged a final judgment. Souls already in heaven, and those still living on earth will enter into heaven after the final judgment, will be reunited with their body.

As to what happens immediately upon our death, I believe most of us contemplate, often in fear. We are not taught by God what happens between the time we die, and our soul leaves the body while we are awaiting our fate through the judgment of God.

What I would choose to believe about that time is that when our soul leaves or body after death (like Jesus, our soul is suspended in darkness for 3 days). We are drifting in a dark abyss. We may even call to mind that beautiful prayer;

The Lord is my shepherd; I shall not want.

He maketh me lie down in green pastures. He leadeth me beside still waters.

He restoreth my soul: He leadeth me in the paths of righteousness for His name's sake.

Yea, though I walk through the shadow of death, I will fear no evil: for Thou art with me;

Thy rod and thy staff comfort me. Thou preparest a table before me in the presence of mine

enemies; thou anointest my head with oil; my cup runneth over. Surely goodness and mercy

shall follow me all the days of my life: and I will dwell in the house of the Lord forever.

In these 3-days of darkness, before our soul is raised and judged, we may feel lonely and

Isolated or forsaken, If we have spent our time on earth working for Christ, time with Him in prayer and meditation, asking for Him to increase our trust, we may spend those 3 days in anticipation and joy knowing that Jesus will be reaching out for us shortly to guide us on our journey home.

Jesus Loves And Calls Each Of Us To Him

As Catholics, we see, hear, and understand God in different ways. Today, I want to share with all, a faith experience I have lived. My husband and I were spending time in Florida for about a month. In the backyard, my husband spent time building a canoe. Inside, I wanted to try my hand at doing a painting. For days I attempted to paint, and my attempts were unsuccessful. One day as I sat at a table contemplating what kind of painting to try, I heard the soft voice I knew to be Jesus say; "Why not paint Me?"

Shocked and confused, I replied internally; "Jesus I am not an Artist, I could never paint You. I could do You no justice." Jesus replied; *"I will be with you."* I could not refuse. With an old piece of hard cardboard I had in the house, I viewed a holy picture that hung on the wall of Christ and began the task. As I began painting, I realized I was making some progress. As I continued, it was as though I was watching someone else paint, and was in awe. I painted things I knew alone I could never have accomplished, such as a part in the hair. Most of all, His eyes will follow you whether you stand to His left, or His right. Enjoy! Print out if you can and frame it, do not cover it with glass as it is said to separate us from God.

Note: The original hangs in my bedroom and is not signed as I felt it was the hand of God that guided my hand. Jesus is so humble, He did not select a famous talented Artist but commissioned me. This is not about the artist but is about God.

Jesus Knows Our Hearts

As we contemplate life after death, we all have images and ideas of our eternal life with God in heaven. In so doing, it is very difficult to imagine all the earthly delights that we must leave behind. For me personally, the idea of never having a dog, or seeing the birds and listening to them sing is sad. I have always felt a kinship with animals. They are loving, loyal, and dependent upon us for their food and love. And because heaven is meant to be joy and peace, I believe that when God said; "I go before you to prepare a place for you", each one of us will enjoy the good things of life on earth that we enjoyed on earth. God knows our hearts intimately, and He wants us to be happy with Him in heaven forever.

Sometimes, our lack of knowledge and understanding of God may cause us to be very sad about leaving this world, our families, and our pets. God knows our hearts, and He will not allow room for sadness in our eternal home.

We may at times, wonder if all of our friends and families, even ourselves will make it to heaven. God knows our hearts and is more than prepared to ease our minds and give us the joy He has planned for us. We would be wise to always add to our prayers, a request that God fills our hearts with enough trust in Him that we never doubt or question His capabilities or plans for us. Therefore, we must leave our apprehensions and uncertainties where they belong, in our emptied bodies back on earth.

It is good to remind ourselves that God knows our human hearts as He created them. We never planned on coming into this world, being born to our parents, and we are not the creator who plans our exit. Only love and trust in His will can bring us the peace and joy our creator had intended for us. Faith, we can be reminded, is believing without knowing. Believing is an action word, and when we are not on guard, the Evil One loves to creep inside of us and create doubt, confusion, and fear.

I pray that each day we awake, we look for God in our hearts, on our walls, and thank Him for another day that we can spend working for Him, and nurturing our relationship with Him. Amen

Speaking of the Devil

Although we do not want to "get to know him", we do want to understand his evil and cunning ways so that we are not caught off guard. "Lucifer" means "light-bearer" and is most associated with a high-ranking angel who fell from heaven and God's grace because of his pride and rebellion against God.

As a fallen angel, we understand that Satan's ability to tempt and to trick people is explained in part, due to his falling from grace and his nature. Although God created Lucifer, now referred to as Satan, or the evil one, as good, Satan became evil by his own doing.

Ironically, his fall is best described as a result of how he made choices through free will and pride. *This information provides us with the knowledge to use our free will wisely in making choices and be reminded that self-pride not used properly, or in excess leads to sin, a fall from God's grace.*

In the Book of Isaiah (14: 12-15) The fall of Lucifer, although not clearly about Satan but rather a taunt against a

Babylonian King. However, Christian tradition has interpreted this passage as an allegory for the fall of Satan.

In the Book of Ezekiel (28: 12-19) Here we find a lament over the King of Tyre, which has also been interpreted allegorically to refer to the fall of Satan due to pride.

In the Testament of Matthew 4:3, Satan is referred to as the "tempter", and Jesus speaks of Satan as "a murderer from the beginning, not holding to the truth, for there is no truth in him.

John (8:44) In these passages, it is mentioned that there is a belief that Satan's power lies in deception and temptation, leading God's people away from Him.

The Catholic church teaches that while Satan has the power to tempt, he does not have the power to force anyone to sin; rather, he influences the will toward evil. The church also affirms that God permits diabolical activities for reasons that are mysterious, yet ultimately serve His just, and merciful plan. And in everything, God blesses the work of all who love Him (**Romans 8:28).**

Book of Revelation, Chapter 20, There is a mention of **1,000 years.** This chapter describes an angel coming down from heaven, seizing the dragon, the ancient serpent, which is the devil or Satan, and binding him for 1,000 years. It states that Satan is thrown into the Abyss, which is to be released for a short time.

This passage is often interpreted as part of the eschatological narrative, which deals with the end ties and the final judgment. The **1,000 years** mentioned in Revelation is commonly **referred to** period. Some see it as a literal thousand-year reign of Christ on Earth, others interpret it symbolically, representing a long period of peace and righteousness.

Finally, it is important to note that the text does not describe this period as a time given specifically for Satan to win over God's people but rather as a time when he is restrained from deceiving the nations. The focus of the passage is more on the reign of Christ and the blessedness of those who take part in the first resurrection.

May is the Month Dedicated to Mary Our Mother

In thinking of our beautiful heavenly Mother Mary, and the Mother of Jesus, I am reminded of sweet-smelling flowers and the rosary. It is true for all of us who have faith and practice our faith that we will, or at some time in our lives, have experienced a mystical moment through that faith within us.

In fervently praying the rosary daily, there was a time in my life upon saying the rosary alone in my bedroom, the smell of sweet perfume filled the air. After completing the rosary, I felt as though I should check for spilled perfume somewhere near my Vanity table. However, as I began to check out the Vanity, I soon became aware that I was completely out of any perfume at all. The hairs on my neck stood up as I recalled reading at one time or another how those who remain faithful to her rosary may at some time, smell her sweetness for she is near.

Our lady appeared to the children of Fatima for the first time on May 17th, 1917, and on each 17th of 6 consecutive months. May in the Catholic church was always dedicated to Mary, the Mother of God, and was celebrated with a "Crowning of Mary," symbolized by a procession of children all dressed in white, symbolizing her purity, and completed with an 8th-grade student who went up into the altar and crowned the statue of Our Lady. I remember vividly being that 8th-grade child who had the good fortune of crowning the Blessed Virgin Mary in May. In those days, Catholic Schools were in every community, and children were all taught by the nuns.

May is dedicated to Mary, the Mother of God in, Catholic tradition. This tradition became widespread during the 19th century. It's a time when special devotions are organized each day throughout the month, including the daily recitation of the Rosary. There are erections of special altars, and the crowning of Mary's statue, a tradition known as "May Crowning". These practices are meant to honor Mary's virtues and serve as a reminder for the faithful to emulate her faith, obedience, humility, and love. Let's pray together for world peace and for the poor souls in Purgatory.

Vacillating Our Trust In God

This topic of trusting in God seems to be a topic, not unlike many others where I believe most of us are very similar. An exception I have noticed at times, appears to be those who leave this world as a Saint.

We grow up learning about God, and the three persons in one God. Although we may have a lack of understanding of this fact, we accept it as part of our faith. We grow in our faith, and we believe our Creator is and always was. Still, as human beings who are imperfect, we have our fears regarding life and, most especially, death.

I am referring most especially to our death and departure from this life and into the next. Often, when things are going well in our lives, we trust in God, He is watching over us. But, when those dark clouds pass over us, such as the loss of a loved one, or we are troubled, possibly, about our own health, our trust may become challenged. Some of us may try to bargain with God with prayers such as, "God, please give me more time and I will get it right, I will be a better person." Our trust in God is critical. We may make promises to God that some will never keep.

It has been written that many of us will cry, beg, bargain, and ask God to spare us if, or when, we feel our life here on earth may be ending. We all realize that life is a terminal state; we all will note that people pass through this life and often are taken very early on in their lives.

Trust in God is the biggest part of our faith. Believing that we will not die, but be risen as was Jesus and live in heaven for all eternity. Why does our trust vacillate and how can we increase our trust in Christ?

It is my opinion, that our trust wavers in God because we believe that we can remain in control of our life and our destiny. This is true while knowing that God is our creator. Therefore, as I have learned, and will share with you; It is only when we submit to the will of God that we can give up our false sense of security. When we "Let go and Let God," we begin to feel God's merciful grace flow through us and find that our trust in God is increasing.

In reading stories regarding some of the Saints, I marveled at how they prayed for God to take them from this world, not because they were ill, but simply because they longed to be with Him. That is true trust. Simple steps that required a daily focus on Christ.

The Stars In The Sky

The stars light the night and are set in order by God. In a message my heart received once from God, He told me that I was like a bright star in the sky and that He named each star in the sky and knew each by name. I thought that perhaps, it was not Jesus speaking to me, but my brain. When returning home from Mass, I went directly to my bible and tried to understand how I could have heard a message from Jesus that I could not make sense of. *There are many times after receiving Holy Communion when in my pew, kneeling, I cover my face to avoid all distractions, and that is when I may hear a few words that come directly from God.*

Searching His words in my Catholic bible, I did not want to share these words until I could satisfy myself that the words were true. As for myself, I had never learned about how God named each star in the sky.

The following verses showed me that God was speaking to me and that I had not been deceiving myself into believing.

In the Catholic Bible, this verse mentions God naming the stars and knowing them all by name is found in **Psalm 147:4.** The verse states: "He determines the number of stars; He calls them each by name."

Philippians 2:15 it states:

"…so that you may become blameless and pure, children of God without fault in a warped and crooked generation." Then you will shine among them like stars in the sky"

This verse encourages believers to live righteously and stand out morally in a world that is often seen as corrupt or misguided. By doing so, they will shine brightly, like stars, as examples of goodness and purity.

The symbolism of a bright star in the sky often represents **divine guidance, hope,** and **prominence**. For instance, the Star of Bethlehem is one of the most famous examples of a star as a divine guide, leading the Magi to Jesus' birthplace. In a broader sense, stars symbolize the light of God's wisdom shining in the darkness, guiding and providing hope. Additionally, stars can represent the glory and splendor of God, as well as the promise of eternal life, as seen in **Daniel 12:3: "**Those who are wise will shine like the brightness of the heavens, and those who lead many to righteousness, like the stars forever and ever."

We Are Not Born Into Sainthood

Many of us have a special Saint that we may have prayed to, and we honor him or her because of the documented life they lived. As Catholics, our self-chosen Confirmation name must be selected from one of the Saints' names. We understand that a Saint is an individual, man or woman, who has demonstrated a holy, selfless life. After documentation after one's death, the process of Canonization may begin to declare a particular individual as a Saint.

We are all called to be holy, to live a life that imitates what Jesus taught us through His life and teachings. In other words, Saints are ordinary people like us, born with original sin, but focus on God and choose to devote their lives to God. Because of their love of Christ and the time they give to prayer, meditation, the sacraments, and serving God, they are blessed with many graces for their service to God.

Many make the decision early in life to marry and raise a family, and this choice in life requires working and earning a sufficient income to support a family. This decision, therefore, becomes a priority in how our time is spent. Others at a young age are immediately drawn to a life of holiness with God as their focus. Thus, they are more likely to grow deeper in their faith and in their relationship with God sooner than their contemporaries who may have chosen the sacrament of Matrimony.

This is not to infer that a couple raising their children to be God-fearing and loving while working to feed and clothe them cannot live a holy life. Evolving into Sainthood, however, requires love, mercy, compassion, humility, much prayer, and meditation, the type of sacrifice often seen as selflessness such as; frequenting the sacraments, and living only to know Christ and submit to His will.

While not all of us are destined to become Saints, we are all called to be holy. Each of us, regardless of our paths in life, can live a life dedicated to Christ. When we give our best at work on the job, as a Nurse, or Doctor, a Chemist, Grocery Store Clerk, or at home cooking a family meal, when we do all that is required of us in the best way that we know how to, we are serving God.

God sees each of us as we live from one day to the next. When God is pleased with our sharing of our time, talents, and love, He will reward us with graces that help us along the way to continue our good works. Also, when we are confronted with a disability that limits our life as we once knew it, or besieged with pain surrounding a medical diagnosis, God will let us know that He is with us by showering us with acceptance, tolerance, and understanding. None of us, singularly or as a group, can ever outdo God when it comes to loving, giving, and mercy.

Life, of course, is terminal for all of us. Keeping in mind that any material success we might achieve in life is not how we will be judged, nor will it travel with us into the next life, allows us to work each day as though it were our last, in that we seek to find a deeper meaning in life, one that is most pleasing to God. Our motives may be a bit self-satisfying as we are hoping that by our life god will have mercy and lift us up on our last day to spend eternity with Him in heaven.

Lamenting

The word lamenting describes loss, death, or grieving. It can also include disappointment. Sadly, many mothers have lost a child, and there is no greater grief in this world than that. Children have lost a mother. Mother's Day is not always a pleasant day for many of us. The blessed Virgin Mary lost her only son and in a most incomprehensible way.

How we handle our losses and disappointments can be expressed through anger, resentment, or by complaining. However, no one in this world can feel our pain, except us and our God. Friends and distant family often have their difficulties such as financial or health problems, or both. Therefore, they may not be able to provide the comfort and support that we long for.

The good news is that we never have to suffer alone. Jesus is always with us. He wants us to go to Him. To lean on Him. This is because He knows our pain, He feels our suffering, and wants to console us. All He wants in return is for us to acknowledge that He made us because He wants and loves us. We may not hear His voice, as He speaks softly within that private corner of our hearts. Gratefully, He does hear us.

We cannot expect God's comfort, love, and mercy that He wants to give to us when we choose to refuse to go to Him and believe in His love for us.

In The United States Conference of Catholic Bishops **John Chapter 21** ~ Three times Jesus asked Simon Peter "Do you love me?" Simon Peter answered Jesus saying; "Yes, I love you, Lord." Jesus replied; "Then go tend my sheep." The third time Simon Peter said to Jesus "Yes of course I love you, but you know that, you know everything."

Much of the Bible requires interpretation, as life, speech, and understanding were different in the days of Our Lord. In John Chapter 21, I felt that Jesus was saying to Simon Peter, "If you love Me, then you must come to Me and be of service." Jesus was telling Simon Peter to tend His sheep. To minister to His sheep. We are His sheep, and He is the good Shepherd.

Perhaps if we accept our disappointments and losses, go to Jesus for comfort, and busy ourselves in service for God, we will begin to feel the many blessings that God desires very much to give to those who are willing to come to Him?

Relentless

For a clear picture of what is associated with the term "relentless", it might do well to examine a couple of similar words, such as determination and stubbornness. Determination best describes an individual with passion, energy, and a strong desire to succeed. And also, with a desire to become admired and respected. Stubbornness, on the other hand, describes an individual who will not change their viewpoint, or opinion even when provided information and evidence that their understanding of a particular opinion is not compatible with proven evidence provided.

God is said to be relentless, and what are we to derive from that statement? The Catholic Bible contains several Verses from various individuals from the time of Christ, including John one of His Apostles.

John 3:16 "God's relentless love is evident in the sacrificial gift of Jesus for our salvation."

Zephaniah 3:17 "God's relentless love brings joy, peace, and celebration to our lives."

Hebrews 11:1 God's relentless faithfulness encourages us to trust Him even when circumstances seem uncertain.

Knowing our hearts as God does, He gave us all that we needed so that we might be able to understand, appreciate, and return to Him the love and trust that He deserves.

It is not God who allows doubt and fear to the point that we are adamant about whether or not, God loves us and will truly lift us into His Kingdom upon our passing. For that reason, and maybe because we are sinful beings by nature, we fear death. We may question our actions, regret words we may have said to another human being, or do something we are truly sorry for, yet realize that we cannot take it back. What is done can not be reversed.

However, in prayer and meditation with God, we grow in trust, and trust *is* the opposite of fear. This does not happen by any means, because we are so good and worthy. Not at all, it occurs in us because God blesses us with graces such as wisdom, understanding, love, peace, and more!

All that is required of us then *is to spend quiet time alone with Christ!* As little as 10-15 minutes a day with God will change our lives, thinking, and feelings. Who of us does not want to replace fear with trust? Who of us wants to be assured that we might have a peaceful death? God asks little of us, and yes it may be difficult to believe that giving God the time that He truly deserves comes with such great rewards.

Where Are You Going From Here?

It is fair to say that most Catholics will at times in their lives, reflect upon those big decisions and choices they have made during their lives. Most probably, we are attempting to reflect on whether we have made good choices. Choices that God might approve of. This is because, as our lives propel forward, we are realizing that life itself is, as I like to call it, *temporary*.

We realize, too, that our Catholic Bible tells us that there will be a final judgment by God, and we will be sent to either Purgatory, Heaven, or Hell. As young adults, our focus and priorities are centered on education, finding a suitable partner to spend the rest of our lives with, buying a home, and raising children. There is absolutely nothing wrong with our objectives at all, except for how our goals are many, and can often create an imbalance in how we manage our time and priorities.

Four major priorities will follow us throughout our lives, and I believe they take precedence as follows; God, Work, Sleep, and Relaxation. As we begin to mature into adulthood, we recognize that without God, we would not have been born, we would not have our precious families, and we would not have the promise of eternity with God in heaven. Without working, we would be unable to eat every day or plan to own a home. Without our spouse, we may lack motivation to work or strive toward a future full of goals, and with a partner by our side. Hobbies, Vacations, and daily living could become mundane.

To expound on our priority, God, without Him in our lives to go to for comfort, support, guidance, and consolation, we would be living empty lives. We are God's children, and when we make it an everyday practice to spend time with Him, to show Him that we love and need Him, we are graced with blessings such as protection, wisdom, joy, and much more! At our jobs, we are often told how to *manage our time.* The reason is to successfully, become more productive!

Balancing our time and setting priorities requires us not to exclude God from our consciousness, and to spend time with Him each day at Mass, praying, or just talking to Him.

And including Him in our daily lives and praying that He, too, will one day include us in His heavenly Kingdom when our lives come to their last day on earth.

How Will God Prepare For Our Coming?

It might be fair to say that we have all thought about how we imagine heaven will be if and when we leave this world. Praying, and living the Commandments, we all hope that God will take our souls to heaven for all eternity.

The question we hold in our hearts are seemingly endless; "Will we have our own little home, and if so, do we sleep? Will we see our loved ones? Will our deceased pets be there? What will we do with our time?"

We know we will be judged on how we lived the Commandments He gave to the Disciples to be handed down to us. **In Mark 12;30 It is written,** "You shall love the Lord your God, with all your heart, with all your soul, with all your mind, and with all your strength."

Mark 12:31 The Second part is this as written: "You shall love your neighbor as yourself. There is no other Commandment greater than these."

Therefore, it is quite clear that we will be judged according to the love, empathy, respect, and offerings we desire from others. The greatest treasure we can give to God is all our love, respect, and obedience. With our neighbor, we can love and respect, especially to all who show us love and respect.

Will we have our abode in heaven? This does seem to be a bit of a mystery. However, God did say; "I go before you to prepare a place for you." Perhaps we will. Many of us are curious about whether or not we will ever see our family and pets again who have gone before us. Most of us are in agreement; however, we will see our parents, our siblings, and our relatives who have gone before us, of course, only if they are in heaven. Our prayers are always heard, and having Masses said for our deceased family members is an act of love.

Will we see our loving pets again? Another mystery that is not answered for us. Yet, we are fine with hoping that we will see them again. God is loving and giving, and He knows what pleases us. Therefore, we can hope and believe that we will.

A last question we often wonder about is how we will spend all of our eternity in heaven, what will we be doing? Again, we can only imagine. Knowing that heaven is peaceful and joyful and everything is much more vivid in heaven, including music, colors, and more, we will be feasting our eyes, especially being in the presence of God. Moreover, we might easily see ourselves visiting old friends and family. And also, sitting by the water listening to the sound of birds, and watching flowers open up in front of our eyes.

Reverence And Gratitude

There is a topic that I want to share with you as it has been growing within me. As I always say, *Life is terminal,* and as we mature and age, we come to appreciate each new way we are given. It is another opportunity to be grateful.

Yes, our opportunity to become grateful. Grateful for each opportunity to make amends to those we may have hurt, to make peace with a renewed acceptance of God's will, and to love all who cross our paths offering friendship. To frequently visit the sacrament of Reconciliation and Holy Communion. Moreover, going to the altar to receive the most sacred body and blood of Jesus Christ, His offering to all of us, is our opportunity to accept His body and blood with reverence and gratitude.

Over the years, I have learned how to be present for that very moment when we swallow the Host and Jesus' heart is joined with our own heart, and I do this by placing my elbows on the back of the pew in front of me and covering my face with both hands. In this way, I am never distracted and can better commune with Christ. To listen and to feel this holy moment with all of my senses. After instituting this practice many, many years ago, there soon were those occasions when I felt my heart race, a new warmth within my chest, and an affirmation of the presence of Christ!

When we take the Host and kneel, yet continue to watch others taking the Host and walking past us, we are not giving Jesus our total attention, the attention and focus that He deserves. My CCD Class ending the beginning of the month (May). And one of my students an altar server happens to sit one pew behind me diagonally. And it warms my heart to notice that she, a 5th Grader, now mimics what she watches me do after receiving the body and blood of Jesus Christ.

I share this today with all as I know that in practicing this way of communing with Jesus, you may find more joy in receiving Him into your body, mind, and soul.

Who is God, And How Do We Best Relate To Him?

This is a topic, I believe, because of God's mystifying essence, we do not know how to relate to Him, other than through our human nature. That is either male or female. And because we are human beings, we are incapable of understanding the power and abilities that belong only to our creator. Many passages in the Catholic bible refer to "God the Father, God the Son, and God the Holy Ghost." We are taught to believe that there are three persons in One God.

Because we have not seen God, and God the Son took on a human form to come down to Earth to sacrifice His life to save us, we inevitably depict Jesus as man, as he did come to us in human form. Yet this is not to say that Jesus cannot take on or have other forms, for He is God. "The Father is in Me as I am in the Father."

The Catechism of the Catholic Church states that "God transcends the human distinction between sexes. He is neither man nor woman: He is God."

In Isaiah 42:14 compares God to a woman in labor.

Isaiah 49:15 and 66:13 liken God's tenderness to that of a mother consoling her child.

Psalms 22 10-11 and Isaiah 66:9 depict God as a midwife.

Our Pastor reminded us of this interesting fact in his Homily this past Sunday. A fact that I had known, yet was tucked away in the back of my mind as I had not reflected on this mystery for some time.

God is beyond time, hours or minutes; He is beyond being categorized as a specific gender. God we know can be anywhere and everywhere within the same moment. There are so many faith mysteries regarding our creator, our God. We, as His creatures, do know of His existence, and to know Him (yes Him), we must accept those mysteries as part of our faith.

We also refer to Him as male because of many parables in the Bible, such as; Jesus referring to His Father in Heaven who sent Him to us to be sacrificed on the Cross and to save us from our sins. We have been taught that there are three persons in One God: God the Father, God the Son, and God the Holy Ghost. Therefore, it is natural for us as human beings to refer to Him as "him" as He came to us in flesh and blood like us.

It is also important to occasionally reflect upon God and what we know He encompasses. And remember that God can do all things, be all things, and be in all places. He sees each of us and knows our hearts' truest feelings.

From God To You

Have you ever reflected on how to hear God speaking to you? We know from shared stories of Saints and visionaries that an audible sound is not heard. Understandably, this concept is difficult for us to conceive of. Yet I can explain that to you as one who has *heard* God's words of guidance. It usually only occurs after years of prayer and meditation while in the state of grace without sin, or when one has received the /sacraments of Reconciliation and Holy Communion.

When God speaks to us it can occur in a couple of direct ways. One way is while praying and talking to God. Then we become quiet and listen. A clear and rapid sequence of words passes through our mind and heart that is not something we were thinking of. The thoughts (words) are enlightening. They are profound and guiding. They provide hope and we realize they came from a greater power than what lies within us. We, as a result, experience joy and excitement realizing *that God hears us and wants to communicate with us. His messages are always meant to be* shared because His messages are not for the messenger alone but for all of His faithful.

Another way God may speak to us is when we are in conflict regarding a specific problem in our lives where we can find no peace or resolution. We pray to God earnestly, and then in His time, we feel we have been given an answer to our dilemma, and we feel a sense of peace come over us. We recognize God is leading us. Also, we may have experienced a sudden sense of peace and joy being in the company of one who has been graced with God's graces and blessings of peace, joy, and understanding.

We need never envy or doubt those who have been blessed with a true and continuous devotion to God. As we mature in our faith and understanding of God and what He desires of us, we all will come to realize that God loves all of His people, and those blessed with graces and gifts through their devotion to Christ are blessed for a very special reason; that reason is to evangelize and share with others what God is waiting and wanting to give to them.

God created all and came to Earth to save all. Many are called but few are chosen. Those who are not chosen are those who are proud and not fully submissive to the will of God. God *is* Love, Mercy, and Humility. Those who truly love God first and above all will imitate His ways until they become their ways.

God Visits In Many Shapes And forms

An encounter with God, I believe, happens every day to different people in separate instances, both here and in faraway places. Reflecting on this concept is actually as simple as a dying person seeing a golden Chariot coming to collect him. Sitting on a beach in the early evening and watching a sunset can often cover us with a blanket of understanding and peace. God is always there for us, it is therefore, we who are not opening the door, making time, and seeking Him to spend time with.

A story as told to me by a family member at one time (and for anonymity, I will call him Johnny) went like this; He was in church and kneeling in prayer, and that is when Johnny noticed an elderly man across the aisle and in a pew closer to the Altar. The man seemed to be in a bit of either physical or spiritual distress as he sat bent over with his right arm holding his head. Johnny felt some concern and empathy. Wanting to do the right thing, he stood up and proceeded up the church aisle toward the man. He lightly tapped him on his shoulder, saying, "Are you alright?" When the elderly man turned his head to look up and face Johnny, he almost fell backward. Johnny said he was shaken and not prepared for the face that was looking up at him. Johnny was startled because of the man's eyes that looked up at him. He felt he had never seen eyes like those before. As best he could describe them was to say they looked Saintly, and not of this world. The elderly man thanked him for his concern, and Johnny went back to his pew, where he sat in bewilderment, asking himself, "What just happened here and now in this church?"

God said, "What you do for the least of my brethren, you do unto Me." In God's words, teachings, and possibly through a life experience, we may become mystified, and rightfully so. By taking a step forward in following God's word and His example through practicing acts of love, mercy, and empathy, we are opening the door and bringing God into our lives, bodies, and hearts.

Another way to experience love for all our brothers and sisters is to realize that we are all created equal, each of us will need that love, empathy, assistance, and mercy from one who is unknown to us, and to preserve faith in humanity that God has created. It is the way God wants us to live.

Forgive Yourselves, As I Have Forgiven You

We Catholics who are faithful to the word of God become the pillars of the church. By that statement, I am saying, we have learned many life lessons, and have found the greater meaning of life to become a faithful servant to Christ. To convey to our children and grandchildren an example that can spare them the disillusionment and regret of using our will in choosing some of Satan's temptations. Desiring luxury, money, sex appeal, new cars, compliments, and so on, and so on.

Realizing at some point in our lives that we often made shallow, meaningless, and selfish choices, we also begin to realize the greatest sin of all that we commit is the hurt that we have caused our Creator, our God, and our Savior. At that point, we make a 180-degree turnaround, and at a fairly early time in our lives as well.

Committed to God, we faithfully attend the Sacraments, follow the Commandments, and work toward becoming pleasing in the eyes of God. We teach our children a bit as God did for us, through good examples.

This does not, however, complete the perfect picture as we still have a demon pursuing us. That demon lies deep within our souls. Although God, in his infinite love and mercy, forgives all who profess sincerity and retain regret and sorrow for having offended Him time and again, it is we who find it difficult within our hearts to forgive ourselves. We often desire to punish ourselves, and this is a big mistake. God has forgiven us! It is Satan once again who lurks in the corner of our hearts and is attempting to keep us from God.

Satan's mission is to whisper into our hearts and minds that we have offended God greatly, and He does not want us. We are not good enough to go to God, and we unfortunately agree with Satan. The truth is that none of us are good enough to go to God. Yet God Himself has provided a way for us to remove sin through the sacrament of Reconciliation when we are sincerely sorrowful for having offended Him. He wants us to be able to come to Him because of His great love and mercy for us. He created us out of love and came to Earth to sacrifice His body and blood to save us. If *that* is not true love, what is? We must love our neighbor as we love ourselves for the love of God.

Our Family

In this world of imperfection, longings, losses, and needs, we are often abandoned by the very children we accepted, loved, and raised. This is indeed often felt like an undeserved punishment. When we are feeling this way, we might ask ourselves, "Did God deserve the physical, emotional, and spiritual punishment He received from His children?" Of course not, He created us out of love.

How then must we accept and view our desertion? We must attempt to reconcile with our children, regardless of how we have been hurt. And if they reject our attempts to love them and receive love in return, we can only tell them that we will always love them and move forward with our lives. In our faith and our churches, many have a lot of love to give, and a need to be accepted. We have a deep appreciation for those who love God with their whole heart and soul.

When we are rejected by a parent, a spouse, or an adult child it can be very painful. Yet, we may have to accept this rejection and move forward with our lives. There is pain in rejection and isolation, and we may even feel we are just not worthy of a family. God sent those people into our lives, and it was a gift from God. Yet free will allows us to either accept or reject.

Spending too much time admonishing ourselves, or others for not sharing our need to have them in our lives puts us into a state of negativity, anger, and more. It also takes us away from the love of God who stands before us with open arms.

A Traditional Scope of Family would include mom and dad, and children of these parents. In a broader scenario, the family also includes aunts, uncles, cousins, and also grandparents.

The New Testament goes even further to include "Believers" as part of God's spiritual family. Through faith, we are **adopted** into God's family. God becomes our **Father,** and **Jesus** is our **Brother.**

This spiritual family transcends ethnicity, gender, and social standing. It is a unity that reflects God's love for humanity.

In conclusion, we are taught that our family has both biological and spiritual connections. This shows us how God's involvement equalizes relationships and transcends diversity as we become united in Christ.

The Holy Spirit

As young Catholics, we have learned about the three persons in One God: The Father, the Son, and the Holy Spirit. We also learned that the Father (God) sent His only Son Jesus Christ down to earth to be sacrificed and to save us from our sins. The Holy Ghost, however, we have not learned too much about, but we know the Holy Spirit is within us all at the time of our Baptism. The Holy Spirit, or Holy Ghost, inspires us, and leads us on our spiritual journey,

Although we accept our faith as it is written and foretold by Jesus' disciples in our Catholic Bible, there are still questions we all have regarding the mysteries of our faith, such as our chemical mixture encompassing body, mind, heart, and soul.

Is our soul tangible? How does the Holy Ghost interact with our souls? How do we keep our souls on track and without the blemishes caused by sin? With some reflection and inner guidance, I have made some human bodily chemistry associations.

Body: Composed of flesh, blood, bones, and many organs, my focus is drawn to the heart. Several times, I have read a short story regarding how a young person nearing death has received a new heart transplant from a donor. One young man met with the young donor's mom a few months after surgery. She wanted to listen to her son's heart beating in the chest of another young man, the receiver of the heart. In conversation, the mother mentioned how her son enjoyed pizza and a few beers every Saturday night. This revelation rocked the receiver of the heart transplant as he never liked the taste of beer at all, and never drank of it. That is not until after his new heart was implanted. There have been a few other stories as well that are quite similar. This information leads us to question whether the heart has a memory. Songs such as; *"Heart and Soul, I fell in love with you."* Is the soul housed within the heart?

Heart; The heart is housed within the body, and dependent upon oxygen to regulate the heart, energy, and so forth. As far as I know, the last organ to function within the body is the heart. When the heart stops beating, we are declared dead.

Mind; Our mind stores much information such as old, new, good or bad, and many learned educational subjects. Our minds review choices and circumstances. and responsible for deciding on our course, making decisions. One might even say the body is the symbol of the Father in that it has many branches. Branches such as the heart, the mind, and many connected organs. The Son, Jesus Christ, might be associated with our heart and soul and part of the body just as Jesus is in God the Father, and God the Father is in Jesus.

The Soul: Just where is our soul? If it is in our body, where is it exactly? And how does the Holy Spirit interact with our souls? And if the Holy Spirit is not interacting within us, or with our souls, what is preventing that from happening?

A spiritual theory resulting from my reflection. To make sense of some of the above types of self-questioning, and be able to "tie things together". I share what could be a possibility.

Tying it all together, The body, mind, and heart are all connected as one entity, similar to the Father, Son, and the Holy Ghost. Where then might our soul, our spirit, be housed? Could it be that the soul is housed within the heart, and is the very root of the tree?

What might interfere with the Holy Ghost's ability to live within our souls? Could that be because our heart (where our soul is housed) is divided? Dependent and loyal to its earthly body? The body has the mind, where it can make choices and decisions, and our heart is very accustomed to allowing the body and mind to make choices and decisions that often separate us from the Holy Spirit. The heart fears death and remains loyal to life, and that can dampen the spirit that lives within us in our very hearts.

How can we succeed in uniting our soul (our spirit) with that of the Holy Spirit? Perhaps if we could override the mind that can make good or bad choices that affect our overall being, we might consider offering our spirit in submission to the Holy Ghost. Paradoxically, for the first time, we could become truly free! Free to trust in the Holy

Spirit, trust in Jesus Christ, and trust in God. Be willing on that final day when the heart stops beating, to flee into the arms of the Holy Spirit and feel the freedom and joy of ascending into heaven to meet our Creator, God Himself.

When God Brings Us To Our Knees

God watches over us and is aware of how we live the life He has given us. When intervention is needed, God will often intercede and point us in the right direction. Sometimes in our lives, we feel that life is good, and is going exactly as we have planned it. We feel that we are strong, capable, and happy.

However, life is just a day at a time. At some point in our lives, we may encounter a great loss, rejection, illness, or financial distress. We find it difficult to understand this sudden turn of events, and we know not where to go for understanding and support. We may be facing more stress and vulnerability than we have ever experienced before. Some will question themselves asking, "Why is this happening to me, and why now?"

This is a perfect time for God to intervene, and He often does this because we have not given God any time in our lives, we were feeling happy, in control, and followed our will in making choices in our lives. Yet our choices led us down a dead-end alley.

We had never thanked God with sincere gratitude for our health or our happiness. We had gotten used to patting ourselves on the back and believing that we were the perfect captains of our ship.

The stresses and strife of life eventually visit each of us at one time or another; however often comes unexpectantly. Perhaps we find ourselves on our knees asking God for His help. We were not comfortable in doing this as it was a new experience for us. We had never been on our knees before asking God to help and lead us.

Could this be God's doing? Is God reaching down to help teach us humility, and letting us realize that we do need Him? He may be helping us more than we realized during this period of stress. He is teaching and leading us that we do need our creator, and it is only He who can lead and guide us in a positive and meaningful way.

Although God gave us free will to make whatever choices in our lives, our free will is often our worst enemy. It can be influenced by Satan or our selfish pride. As I like to remind myself occasionally; *Life is terminal.* God's love and mercy are *eternal!* Using our will is not free because it can be associated with sinfulness. God wants us to submit our will to His will. That is the wisest choice we can ever make in our lives.

Opening Our Hearts, Allowing Peace to Enter

Life does not always go as planned for any of us. We are met throughout our lives with issues over which we seem to have no control. This is especially true for those of us who are individuals who have difficulty accepting that we are not in control. Yet, accidents or illness can befall anyone at any time. Maybe a loss of income due to a layoff, divorce, or even an estranged adult child seems to constantly nag at our thoughts and tug at our hearts. We tend to go over and over in our minds the events leading up to our crisis, we examine again and again, the idea that this happened due to our negligence. Acceptance and moving forward seem to be beyond our capabilities.

When we profess with our thoughts, feel in our hearts, and verbalize that we truly put God first in our lives, why then can we not "Let Go, and Let God?" Carrying our cross and allowing God to help us is a freeing experience. God wants to be there for us, but we must acknowledge and accept that He is always the answer.

When we give our burdens over to God, we are in effect, glorifying Him as our Creator, our Mentor, and our Leader. We open our hearts and allow Him to come in and take over. God is peace, love, and mercy. This is the answer as it allows His peace to flow through us. Acceptance is often difficult because it reminds us we are weak and make wrong decisions without God.

Yet knowing God is at the helm of our Ship, we can travel through the darkness without fear. God knows, hears, sees, and understands our needs. Yet it is we who must show our love and our trust in Him. This is the way we can reap His many gifts of courage, endurance, and understanding. Let us all then, open up our hearts and allow peace to come in.